First-class journey

2586288

D0231134

CREATIVITY ON THE GO
HOLIDAY

Pack a bag, grab your hat,
ask a friend to feed the cat.
Turn the page, what's more to say?
It's time to go on holiday!

This HOLIDAY book
belongs to

....

Around the world ticket

2586288

What's inside this book?

HOLIDAY ART

This book is packed full of dream holiday scenes to spot, match, draw, colour and create!

STENCILS

Look for the stencils inside (hint - go to the back of the book). Then hunt for the pages where you can use them.

STICKERS

Your holiday stickers are at the back of the book. Use them on your sticker scenes or anywhere you like!

THINGS TO MAKE

A cool label for your holiday luggage on page page 21, and scrummy ice cream on page 36. Don't forget to check out the holiday craft paper on page 11.

PUZZLES AND GAMES

There are dot-to-dots, mazes, spot the differences and games. Race along the railway track on page 28, then take your chances with an awesome theme park card game on page 50!

This is a Carlton book
Text, design and illustration
© Carlton Books 2012

Published in 2016 by
Carlton Books Limited
An imprint of the
Carlton Publishing Group,
20 Mortimer Street,
London W1T 3JW

A catalogue record for this book is available from the British Library.

10 9 8 7 6 5 4 3 2 1

ISBN: 978-1-78312-211-0
Printed and bound in China

Author: Mandy Archer
Executive editor: Selina Woo
Art editor: Emily Clarke
Design: Zoë Dissell
Illustrations: Jennie Poh
        & Elle Ward
Production: Claire Halligan

Ticket to ride

It's time to go on holiday! To travel through this book you must have a valid passport! Grab a pen and fill in your details below.

I'm going sightseeing somewhere in this book. Can you find me?

1. Surname _____

2. First name(s) _____

3. Nationality _____

4. Date of birth _____

5. Boy ☐

   Girl ☐

Draw or stick in your photo →

Now you're ready to see some amazing places! Turn the page to pack your bags and choose your holiday buddies.

Let's go on holiday

School's out and you're booked on the best holiday EVER!

Where would your dream destination be? Do you want to play by a pool, camp in the mountains or go on safari?

Decide where you want to go, then draw a holiday snap of yourself here. What will you be wearing?

PACK YOUR STUFF

It's time to pack a few essentials. Place a tick next to the five items that you think will be the most useful.

TRAVEL BUDDIES

Would you take friends, your family or a mixture of the two? Decide who's coming with you, then draw their pictures and add their names here.

Name →

FIND YOUR RIDE

How are you going to get to your dream destination? Think carefully - travelling to Australia will take months by bus! Tick the mode of transport that's best for your journey.

Now write your ticket here. ←

PLAN YOUR ROUTE

You may have chosen your dream holiday hot spot, but do you know exactly where it is in the world? Draw a cross on the map to show where you're travelling to.

POTTY PYRAMID MAZE

This sightseer has taken a fascinating pyramid tour in Egypt, but she's got lost!

Help her find a way back to the exit before the sun goes down.

THE WORLD'S MOST FAMOUS PYRAMIDS STAND IN GIZA, NEAR EGYPT'S NILE RIVER. EACH ONE IS A TOMB FOR AN ANCIENT EGYPTIAN KING.

EXIT

TOUR BUS

The answer is on page 80.

Cruise views

Ship ahoy! What can you see through the ocean liner's porthole?

Draw your view here.

Congratulations!
Only first class passengers get a cabin with a window.

Take a flight

Take a look at these two airport scenes. Can you spot eight differences between them?

The answers are on page 80.

Cycling spot

It looks like these cyclists are having a wonderful biking holiday!

Now take another peep at the picture. There are three things wrong with this scene - can you spot them all?

The answers are on page 80.

9

Holiday paper - and what to do with it!

Four fun things to do with your art paper.

1 Cut out the CLOTHES shapes on the back of your holiday paper. See if you can find the two different activities where they are needed. Grab some glue and stick the clothes where they go best. Hey presto, another job well done!

2 Pick your favourite patterned paper and use it to make amazing FLAGS for sandcastles. Cut out a diamond shape, wrap it round a drinking straw and you'll have the most eye-catching castle on the beach!

3 Use your STENCILS to cut interesting shapes out of the paper, then stick them in a collage on the front of a blank notebook. Cover the shapes in a layer of sticky back plastic. You've just made a designer TRAVEL JOURNAL!

4 Cut out some shapes from the paper. Use them to decorate a POSTCARD from your holiday destination. Now send it to a friend!

Cut out these shapes then find out where they belong

Cut out these shapes then find out where they belong

Beach belles and muscle men

The beach is packed with people today, but it's not fun being on the beach with bits missing!

Stick the paper clothes on these beach bathers!

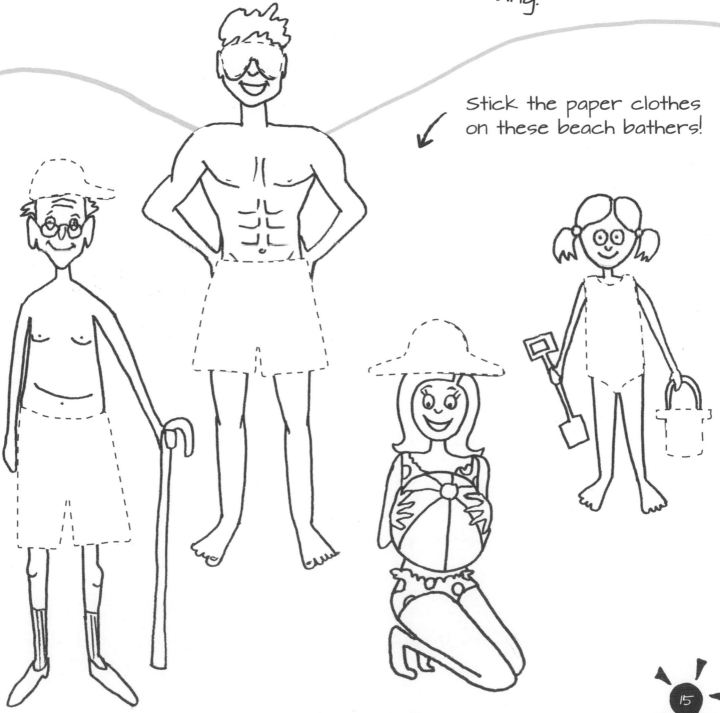

HOLIDAY PHOTOS

You can't go on holiday without a camera!

Look at this fantastic photo of some children on a trip to a city zoo.
Can you answer all of the quiz questions?

Having fun on our
visit to the zoo.

The doggy-shaped balloon is green. Yes ☐ No ☐
The zookeeper is holding a bucket of kippers. Yes ☐ No ☐
The animal in the background is a giraffe. Yes ☐ No ☐
One of the children is laughing at a penguin. Yes ☐ No ☐

The answers are on page 80.

City break!

The world is full of awesome cities!

These holidays photos are packed with sights from some of the most famous places in the world. Study the photos and read the captions, then draw a line to match each shot with the right location.

Took a boat across the Seine to see this sight. Oh la la!

A

The Sydney Opera House, Sydney, Australia

B

The Statue of Liberty, New York City, USA

You could set your watch by this clock!

This gigantic work of art stands on its very own island.

C

The Eiffel Tower, Paris, France

D

Big Ben, London, England

Wonderful views across the Harbour. It's great down under!

17

The answers are on page 80.

Work of art

What great work of art do you think these tourists are jostling to get a look at?

THE FAMOUS LOUVRE MUSEUM IN PARIS, FRANCE HOUSES ALMOST 35,000 OBJECTS AND WORKS OF ART

Draw it in here.

Lazy gazing

Circle eight differences between these rockpool pictures.

One of these marine moochers only appears in the top picture. Which is it?

sea urchin

hermit crab

starfish

19

The answers are on page 80.

Flag it up

Use the pictures and country clues to help you fill in the countries for each of these flags.

Enormous Asian country. Beijing is the capital.

_____

Home to Her Majesty, Queen Elizabeth II.

_____

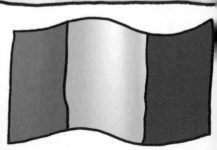

A nation famous for its snowy mountains, watches and chocolate.

_____

A holiday destination surrounded by sunny islands. The largest is Crete.

_____

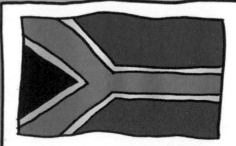

A large African country that hosted the 2010 Football World Cup.

_____

Mediterranean country loved for its pizza, pasta and ice cream.

_____

The answers are on page 80.

Design your own luggage labels

If you don't want your suitcase to get lost, make sure it stands out from the crowd!

These designer luggage labels will make sure that your belongings always end up in the right hands.

Turn over to find out what to do next.

1 Ask a grown-up to help you CUT OUT the labels.

2 Use a pencil to draw an eye-catching PICTURE on the blank sides. You could write your name in giant letters or draw your favourite holiday location.

3 Find some FELT-TIP PENS and colour the design in. Add some GLITTER and STICKERS, too!

4 Write your name and address on the other side.

5 Carefully cover each label with STICKY TAPE, and trim it around the edges. Punch a hole in each label with a hole-punch, then thread a short piece of STRING or RIBBON through it.

Name:

Address:

Contact number:

PLEASE RETURN IF FOUND

6 Tie the labels onto your luggage and you'll be ready to travel in style!

Name:

Address:

Contact number:

PLEASE RETURN IF FOUND

Safari sketches

Lucky you! You're on an amazing safari trip in Africa.

What can you see through your binoculars today?

AFRICA'S BIG FIVE ANIMALS FOR SAFARI SPOTTERS.
1. LION
2. LEOPARD
3. RHINO
4. ELEPHANT
5. BUFFALO

BUT DON'T FORGET ABOUT GIRAFFES, HIPPOS AND GORILLAS, TOO!

Holiday diary

Write your own fascinating travel story.

I can't believe that I've finally arrived in _____

The journey was _____

_____ _____

_____

Once we'd dropped off our bags, I set out to explore. The first thing I came across was _____

_____

_____

Soon I got hungry. I dined on a feast of _____

_____

_____

_____

The rest of the time was spent _____

_____

_____

_____

_____

_____

(_____)

(_____)

_____

_____

_____

_____

_____

What a once-in-a-lifetime experience!

Sandcastle art

Copy this sandcastle onto the empty grid opposite.

26

It's easier if you copy the lines square by square.

Railway races

You and your friend are going on holiday to the seaside. You've both dreamed about buying an ice cream and building a sandcastle on the beach. Who will get there first?

HOW TO PLAY

1. Grab a pal with a sense of adventure, then find two counters and a die.

2. Work your way along the route, taking turns to throw the die and follow the instructions at each stop.

3. The first person to hit the beach is the winner!

If you don't have proper counters, use pennies or old buttons!

START

1

2

First Class Seat 541127

3
Get upgraded to first class. Move forward 2 stops.

4

5

6

7

8

9

10
Jump on a night train. Go to stop 18

11

12
You lose your rucksack. Go back to the start.

13

14

Room with a view

Welcome to your holiday villa! What can you see out of the window?

Draw it here and add some stickers to the scene.

Holiday stencils - and what to do with them!

Look at the back of the book to find your stencils. Tear them out of the book and get creative!

1 Use the stencil shapes on your own STATIONERY, such as letters, birthday cards, party invitations and envelopes.

2 Decorate a row of BUNTING for your bedroom with the stencil shapes. Trace the outlines onto triangles of paper, then fix them to a length of string. Drape the bunting over your pin board or across your bookshelf.

3 Find a large sheet of paper, then stencil yourself a happy holiday POSTER. Colour the shapes in bright shades, then ask a grown-up to pin the poster on the ceiling above your bed. When you wake up in the morning, it will be the first thing you'll see!

4 Make a HOLIDAY SCRAPBOOK, then fill it with old tickets, postcards and photos. Use your stencils to decorate it. Don't forget to date the scrapbook, so you can look back at it in the future.

Pool party!

Let's get this party started!

Find some coloured pens, then use your stencils to fill the pool with happy holidaymakers.

What delicious food is on the tray?

Who is he splashing?

Draw a beautiful beach towel.

Decorate the chairs.

Draw yourself on the slide. Weeee!

Give her a beachball to catch.

Add some splashes!

Learn the lingo

Make up a brand new language for these people to speak.

What name will you give your language and what country is it spoken in?

_____

_____

Souvenir spend-up

You have €5.00 to buy presents for your friends back home.

€0.95

€0.50

€1.20

€2.00

€1.50

Can you afford all of the things on the shelves?

Total = _____

The answer is on page 80.

Slurptastic homemade ice cream

EVERYBODY loves to slurp ice cream when they're on holiday!

This recipe will show you how to make your own simple ice cream you can tuck into all year around.

This recipe makes enough ice cream for you and one lucky friend.

You will need:
2 tablespoons sugar
240 ml full fat milk
½ teaspoon vanilla extract
6 tablespoons rock salt
1 medium zipped plastic food bag
1 large zipped plastic food bag
crushed ice

FULL FAT MILK

sugar

ICE

rock salt

1 medium plastic bag

1 Tip the sugar, milk and vanilla extract into the medium plastic food bag. Mix the ingredients with a spoon and then zip the bag shut.

2 Take the large plastic bag and fill it half way up with crushed ice. Tip in the salt and shake the bag gently.

3 Carefully place the medium food bag into the larger one. Zip the outer bag closed, then give it a good shake.

4 Keep going for at least five minutes until the ingredients in the smaller bag start to blend and thicken up.

5 Lift the bag of ice cream out of the larger ice bag and scoop it into a bowl or cone. Enjoy!

I large plastic bag

To create other flavours, you can swap vanilla extract for:

* A teaspoon of cocoa powder
* Pureed strawberries
* A tablespoon of toffee sauce

Driving dot-to-dot

Who's taking a road trip down Route 66?

ROUTE 66 WAS A 3940-KM ROAD THAT RAN ALL THE WAY FROM CHIGAGO TO LOS ANGELES IN THE USA.

Join up the dots to find out.

ROUTE US 66

38

Jumping jigsaws

Everyone loves a bouncy castle on holiday.
Can you put this bouncy castle back together again?

Circle the jigsaw piece that is missing
from the picture.

 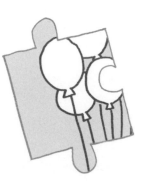  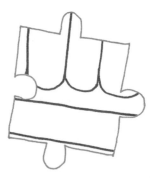

The answer is on
page 80.

Holidaymaker match-up

Can you match each of these tourists to the holidays they have booked?

Draw a line to connect each tourist to the correct holiday.

A Diving in the sea and coral reefs

B Snowboarding in the mountains.

C A camel ride across the desert.

D Sunbathing on the beach.

E Wildlife watching in the woods.

F A visit to art galleries and museums.

The answers are on page 80.

Camper van kid

This surf dude is loading up his camper van for the long summer break.

Help him get ready by finding the stickers that match his equipment below.

A: Sound system
B: Camcorder
C: Flip flops
D: Skateboard
E: Wet suit
F: Boogie board

Give the surfer a cool name, then use your stickers to decorate the outside of his van.

_____

41

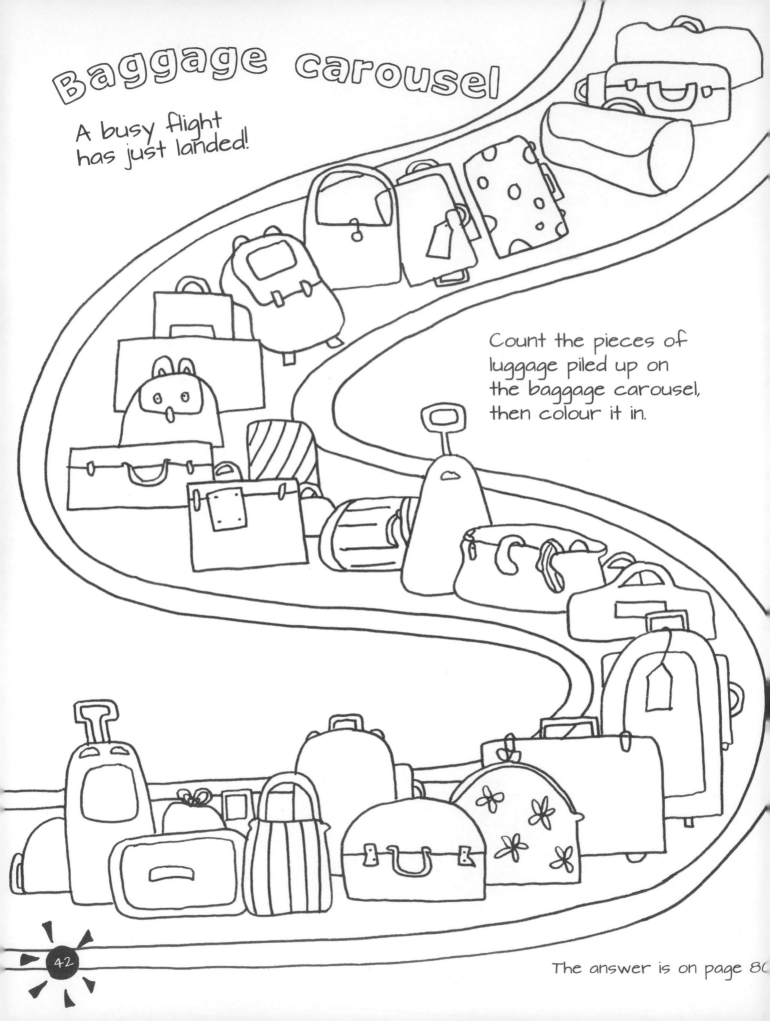

Baggage carousel

A busy flight
has just landed!

Count the pieces of
luggage piled up on
the baggage carousel,
then colour it in.

The answer is on page 80

Mad menus

Some of the meals on this menu are rather exotic!

Take the tick test to decide which ones are genuine dishes from around the world and which ones are false.

NAUGHTY NOSH RESTAURANT

1. Bird's nest soup
   - [ ] True
   - [ ] False

2. Armadillo pie
   - [ ] True
   - [ ] False

3. Fried tarantulas
   - [ ] True
   - [ ] False

4. Snake wine
   - [ ] True
   - [ ] False

5. Meerkat munchies
   - [ ] True
   - [ ] False

6. Reindeer steaks
   - [ ] True
   - [ ] False

43

The answers are on page 80.

postcard writer

Don't go away without sending a few postcards to everyone back home!

Grab a pencil and write a special message to your best friend.

Make the message as exciting as possible. Describe the sights, sounds and smells of the place. Now design a postage stamp to go above the address.

MESSAGE IDEAS
Stuck for inspiration? Give these postcard phrases a try!
- The weather here is...
- The best thing we've done so far is...
- The place that I am staying in...
- The funniest moment was when...
- The food tastes...
- The most eye-popping sight was...

BUY A MAP OF THE WORLD, THEN ASK A GROWN-UP TO PIN IT TO YOUR BEDROOM WALL. NEXT TIME YOU GO ON HOLIDAY, SEND YOURSELF A POSTCARD. ASK YOUR FRIENDS AND FAMILY TO DO THE SAME.

TAPE EACH OF YOUR POSTCARDS AROUND THE BORDER OF THE MAP, CIRCLING THE PLACES VISITED WITH A BRIGHT PEN. CAN YOU COLLECT A CARD FROM EVERY CONTINENT?

Now draw a bright picture on the front of the postcard, showing your holiday destination. You could even add some stickers for extra decoration.

Face-painting fun

At a day out at the fair, these children are waiting to have their faces painted.

Find some bright colours then give each one a crazy new look!

Why not paint an animal face!

Catch a coach

It's time to take a coach tour across France!

Study the coach timetable, then answer the quiz questions at the bottom of the page.

Timetable	Coach 1	Coach 2	Coach 3	Coach 4
Paris	07:14	09:03	10:50	12:35
Orléans	09:24	11:13	13:00	14:45
Bordeaux	14:45	16:34		20:06

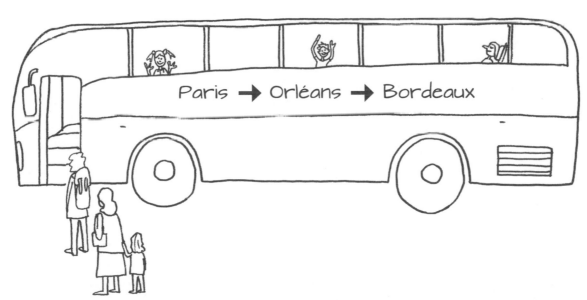

Paris ➡ Orléans ➡ Bordeaux

1 How many coaches go from Paris right through to Bordeaux?

2 What time does the first coach of the day get to Orléans?

3 Your friend is getting on the coach that leaves Paris at 10.50. What time will they get to Orléans?

The answers are on page 80.

Map challenge

Help the holidaymaker find her way around the museum.

The coordinates for the greatest exhibits on show are listed below. On the plan of the museum opposite, put one finger on the letter and another on the number. Then move them together in a straight line until they meet.

Write your discoveries here:

G4 _____

C8 _____

D2 _____

H5 _____

A1 _____

E6 _____

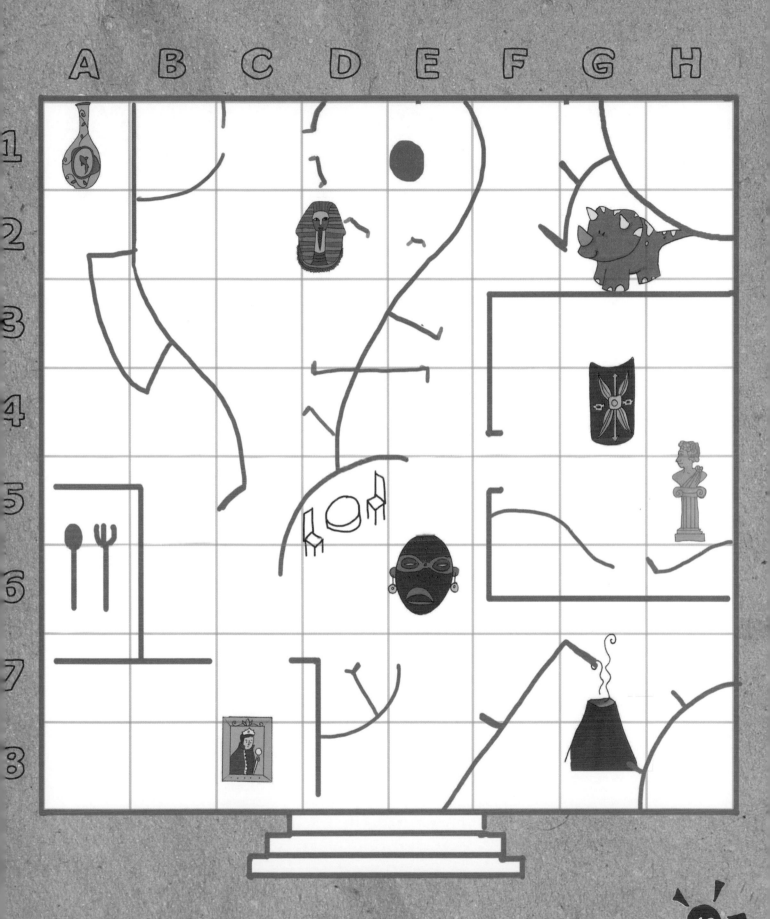

The answers are on page 80.

White knuckle riders
Can you handle every ride in the theme park?

1 CUT out the 18 cards on the following pages, using the dotted lines as a guide. If you want to make your cards extra strong, cover each one with sticky back plastic and trim it to size.

2 Find a friend, then share out the cards so that you have 9 each. The dealer always goes first.

3 Look at the top card in your pack, making sure your rival can't see it. Pick the ride's strongest category (speed, giggle rating or thrill factor) and read out its value. If your opponent's value is lower, take his or her card and add it to the bottom of your stack. If yours is lower, pass your card to the other player. If the value is the same, put both cards in the middle.

4 Whoever wins the round gets to play next. The winner of the next round gets to take their rival's card and all the cards in the middle. When they lose a round, the turn switches to the other player.

5 Keep trading until your cards run out. Which one of you will get their hands on every ride in the park?

6 Once you've got used to playing why not invite a third player to join you, splitting the cards into three equal piles at the start? You could even get creative and make some extra cards to add to the set!

Runaway Train

Speed: 58/100
Giggle rating: 8/10
Thrill factor: 76%

Texas Tornado

Speed: 89/100
Giggle rating: 3/10
Thrill factor: 92%

Scream Machine

Speed: 64/100
Giggle rating: 0/10
Thrill factor: 99%

Tidal Wave

Speed: 35/100
Giggle rating: 9/10
Thrill factor: 78%

Pirate Falls

Speed: 23/100
Giggle rating: 9/10
Thrill factor: 88%

Twister

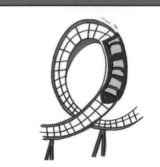

Speed: 83/100
Giggle rating: 9/10
Thrill factor: 84%

Elevator Drop

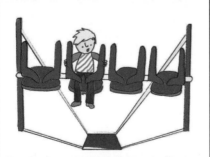

Speed: 100/100
Giggle rating: 2/10
Thrill factor: 100%

Fire-breathing Dragon

Speed: 74/100
Giggle rating: 6/10
Thrill factor: 71%

Raging Rapids

Speed: 46/100
Giggle rating: 9/10
Thrill factor: 85%

Adrenalin Rush

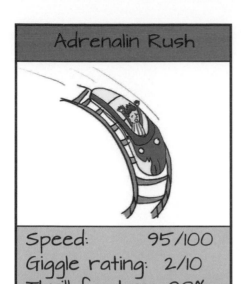

Speed: 95/100
Giggle rating: 2/10
Thrill factor: 98%

Crazy Caterpillar

Speed: 73/100
Giggle rating: 5/10
Thrill factor: 81%

The Monster

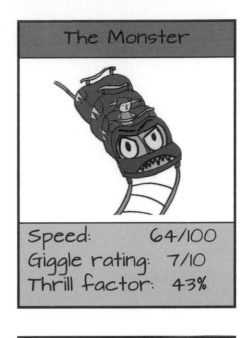

Speed: 64/100
Giggle rating: 7/10
Thrill factor: 43%

Tunnel of Doom

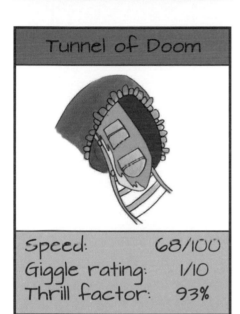

Speed: 68/100
Giggle rating: 1/10
Thrill factor: 93%

Cat and Mouse

Speed: 55/100
Giggle rating: 8/10
Thrill factor: 49%

Neptune's Revenge

Speed: 52/100
Giggle rating: 7/10
Thrill factor: 86%

Flip Trip

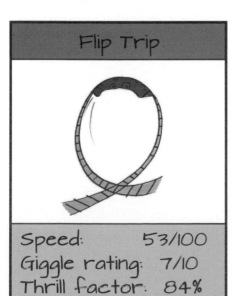

Speed: 53/100
Giggle rating: 7/10
Thrill factor: 84%

Space Attack

Speed: 83/100
Giggle rating: 2/10
Thrill factor: 94%

Goliath

Speed: 96/100
Giggle rating: 4/10
Thrill factor: 100%

pack and go
It's time to pack your suitcase!

Draw your favourite holiday clothes, then stick in some swimwear from pages 11 and 14.

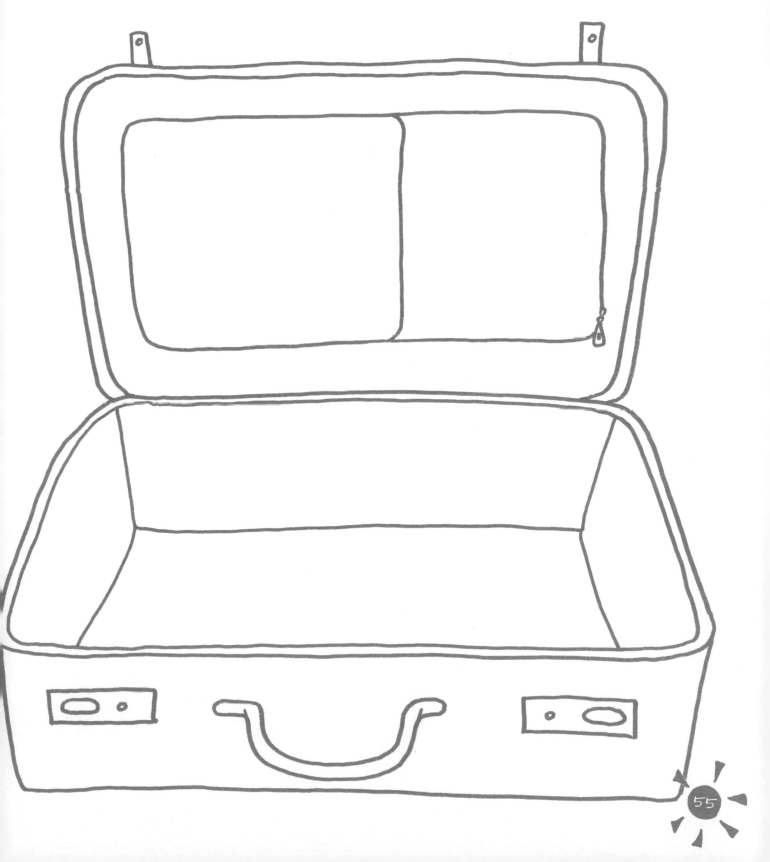

Happy snorkeller

Draw the snorkeller onto the frame opposite, copying over all the colours, too!

House exchange

Try something different this year, organize a house exchange!

If you could swap houses for a fortnight with a family from another country, what kind of home would you choose? Colour them all in!

Native American tepee

Inuit igloo

Kenyan tribal hut

Swiss chalet

Japanese pagoda

Funny food
What will you eat on holiday?

PIZZAS HAVE BEEN EATEN FOR THOUSANDS OF YEARS! EVEN THE ANCIENT GREEKS LIKED TO EAT FLATBREADS TOPPED WITH HERBS, ONION AND GARLIC.

Add some delicious toppings to this pizza. Can you draw the ingredients in a pattern that makes you smile?

My favourite pizza flavour is

_____

Ski slope dot-to-dot

Look who's whizzing down the black run at this ski resort!

Put your pencil on the number '1' then follow the numbers to connect up the dots.

60

The answer is on page 80.

Your favourite holiday book

What do you most like to read on holiday? Design your book here.

title

title

author

picture

author

Holiday things to colour in

Holiday stickers - and what to do with them!

1 Go to the back of the book and find your stickers to complete the puzzles on page 64. Then use them to decorate the fold-out sticker scenes on the last page. Use your stickers again and again.

2 Look out for all the other pages where you can use your STICKERS:

Design your own luggage labels - page 21
Room with a view - page 30
Holiday stencils - page 31
Camper van kid - page 41
Postcard writer - page 44
Sails in the sunshine - page 69
Parade on the pier - page 76
Dream destination - page 78

3 Check with a grown-up, then use the stickers to decorate your pencil tins, passport cover, suitcases, journal, cards, folders and exercise books.

4 Use your stickers to make your POSTCARDS home even more special. Pop in a picture underneath your message. Let your pen pal know that you're writing by putting a sticker on the back of every envelope you mail off.

Beach sticker quiz

 Find the right stickers to get you in the holiday mood.

The only drink to sip beneath the palm trees.

Something delicious to eat by the sea.

The light is so bright, you've got to wear these all day long.

A beach is the perfect holiday location. Think of gentle ocean breezes, white sand and palm trees.

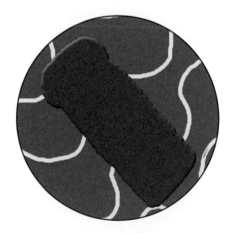

The ultimate accessory for relaxing in the water.

Pull these on, find a snorkel and start exploring!

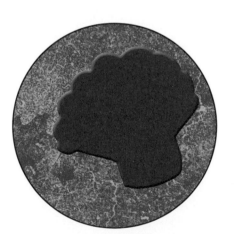

You'll find loads of these all over the beach.

ungle adventure

Take a river trip into the jungle.

olour in the picture,
ing the key to choose
e right shades.

1 = red   4 = purple
2 = yellow   5 = green
3 = brown   6 = light green

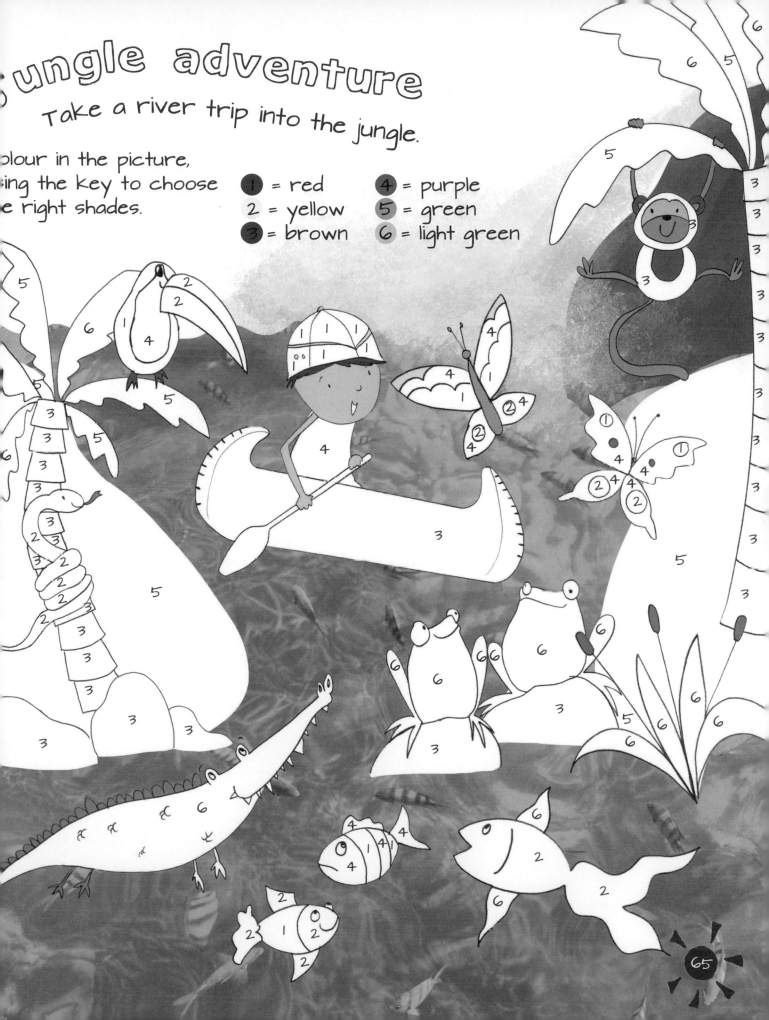

Message in a bottle

Some holiday destinations are so special, visitors try to keep them a secret!

This tourist has even written a message home in code. Use the letter key to help you decipher the message.

Message:

HGZBRMT LM Z IVNLGV
YVZXS, UZI ZDZB UILN
ZMBLMV. MVD AVZOZMW
RH GSV YVHG!

A = Z
B = Y
C = X
D = W
E = V
F = U
G = T
H = S
I = R
J = Q
K = P
L = O
M = N
N = M
O = L
P = K
Q = J
R = I
S = H
T = G
U = F
V = E
W = D
X = C
Y = B
Z = A

_ _ _ _ _ _ _   _ _   _ _ _ _ _ _

_ _ _ _ _,   _ _ _   _ _ _ _   _ _ _ _

_ _ _ _ _ _.   _ _ _   _ _ _ _ _ _ _

_ _   _ _ _ _   _ _ _ _ _!

The answer is on page 80.

Cable car ride

These cable cars are working hard to climb the steep mountain slope.

Only one of the cars is different to the rest - can you spot the odd one out?

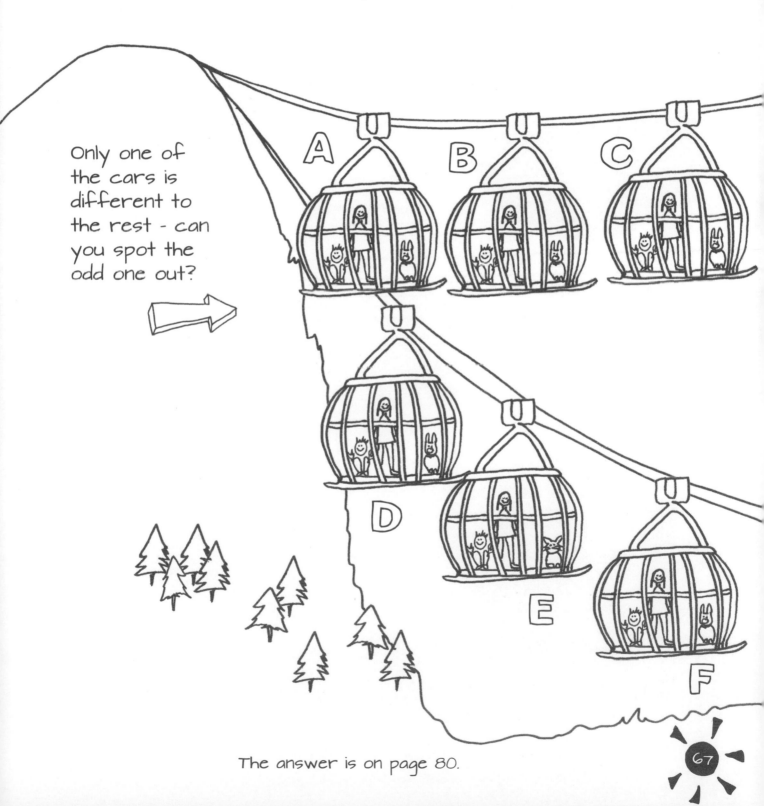

The answer is on page 80.

Sticker puzzle

What's your dream holiday?

Find the stickers that match the holiday scenes.

Camping in the country

Snorkelling in the ocean

Beach party!

City sightseeing

Climbing in the mountains

Sails in the sunshine

These yachts have been sailing around Pineapple Bay all day.

Follow their trails to find out where each of them will be mooring for the night.

Lizard Lagoon

Smuggers' Cove

Black Horse Harbour

The answers are on page 80.

69

Lovely landmarks

Read about these wonders of the world and then colour them in.

Taj Mahal
Not many tourists realise that the stunning Taj Mahal in India is a tomb, rather than a palace. An emperor called Shah Jahan built it in honour of his dead wife.

The Great Wall of China
It has been said that the Great Wall is so big it can be seen from space. This is not true, but it is still one of the most adventurous building projects ever attempted.

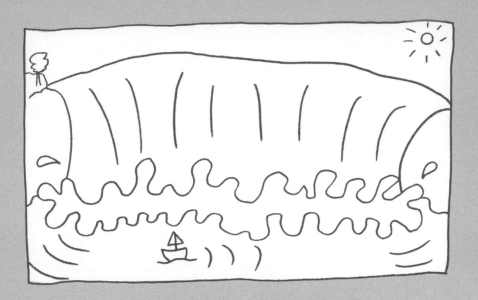

Niagara Falls
These awesome waterfalls gush and roar on the border between Canada and the United States.

Stonehenge
Stonehenge is a strange collection of prehistoric rocks in England. Even today, it remains a mystery. No one knows how our ancestors could have transported and lifted the heavy stones.

The Colosseum
The Colosseum is an ancient amphitheatre in the heart of Rome, Italy. It was built in the days of the Emperors and was where spectators watched fights between gladiators.

zoo crew

What do you think each of these animals should be called?

_____ the meerkat

_____ the python

_____ the gorilla

Take a tour of the zoo, then choose a name to put on the front of each cage.

_____ the panda

_____ the tiger

Mirror mirror!

Draw yourself in your favourite holiday gear here!

Camping chaos

Write a story to connect these crazy camping pictures.

It all started on a blustery day...

_____   _____   _____

_____   _____   _____

_____   _____   _____

_____   _____   _____

The end

Castle count-up

This poor tour guide is supposed to be showing 10 visitors round the castle, but the group has split up!

Can you help him find his lost guests?

Draw a circle around every tourist that you find.

THE METAL GRILLE AT THE ENTRANCE TO A CASTLE IS CALLED A PORTCULLIS.

The answer is on page 80.

parade on the pier
use your stencils, stickers and colouring pens to bring the pier to life.

76

Dream destination

Make a wish list of your favourite holiday places.
How many of them have you visited so far?

1 ....

2 ....

3 ....

4 ....

5 ....

Signed by ....

Now add some stickers to decorate the page.

The Happy Holiday Society

VIP TRAVELLER

This is an official stamp to certify that

_____

has proved themselves to be
a true global traveller.
KEEP ON EXPLORING!

Answers

3 Boy repeated on page 71

6

8

9

16
1 No
2 Yes
3 Yes
4 No

17
A B C D

20
China Greece
United Kingdom South Africa
Switzerland Italy

19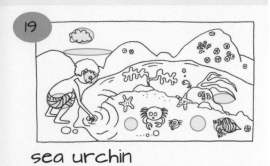
sea urchin

35 Total = €6.15

38

39 Third puzzle piece

40

42 34 bags

43
1. True (China)
2. False
3. True (Cambodia)
4. True (Vietnam)
5. False
6. True (Canada)

47
1. Three
2. 09.24
3. 13.00

48
G4 Roman shield
C8 Portrait
D2 Egyptian mask
H5 Statue
A1 Vase
E6 African mask

60

66 Staying on a remote beach, far away from anyone. New Zealand is the best!

67 E: The animal is different.

69

75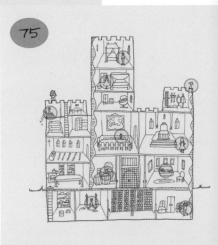